W9-DFI-214

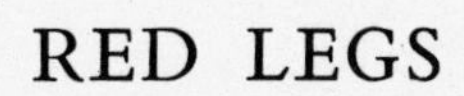

RED LEGS

RED LEGS

by Alice E. Goudey

Illustrated by Marie Nonnast

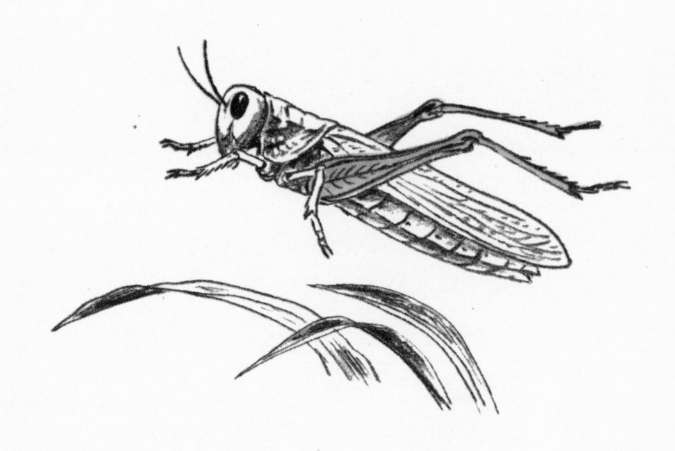

CHARLES SCRIBNER'S SONS • NEW YORK

A—2.66 [RJ]

Printed in the United States of America
Library of Congress Catalog Card Number 66-12548

NOTE

The red-legged grasshopper in this book, is one of our most common grasshoppers. He is found in grassy places almost everywhere in the United States except in the Western mountains. His scientific name is *Melanoplus femur-rubrum*.

There are many other kinds of grass-hoppers. One is the Carolina. This big grasshopper is often seen along the side of dusty roads and for this reason is sometimes called the "dusty-road grasshopper." Some other grasshoppers are the American, the Lubber, and the Migratory.

Some grasshoppers, such as the Little Pygmy, hide beneath the grass and live through the winter. But others, such as Red Legs, die when cold weather comes.

Grasshoppers belong to the large group of animals called *Insects*. One can tell whether or not an animal belongs to this group by counting its legs. If it has six legs, it is an insect.

Grasshoppers can be dreadful pests. In years when they hatch in great numbers, they have been known to cause farmers a great deal of trouble by eating entire fields of grain, grass and vegetables, and even the leaves of trees and bushes.

But they are also useful. They are food for many birds, small mammals, and other animals.

In addition, grasshoppers are such lively little creatures, we like to see them hopping about in fields and meadows and along the roadside. They seem to be a part of summer days.

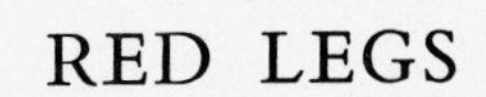

RED LEGS

Down in the meadow
near an old fence post,
thirty tiny grasshopper eggs
lie hidden in the ground.
No one knows they are there.

Anyone could walk over the ground
where the eggs are hidden
and never know
he was walking over
grasshopper eggs.

Little grasshoppers
will hatch out of these eggs—
if hungry, hunting animals
do not find them first.
It is a dangerous world
for grasshopper eggs.

One night
when the moon is round and yellow,
a skunk comes hunting.
The skunk is hungry.
He walks slowly across the meadow,
sniffing the ground.
Suddenly he stops.

He has smelled the tiny eggs.
A skunk likes a supper
of grasshopper eggs.

The skunk
digs a little hole in the ground
and finds the eggs.
He eats fifteen of them.
But before he has time
to eat any more,
a Great Horned Owl,
his wings tipped with soft feathers,
drops noiselessly from the sky.

He frightens the skunk away
from the grasshopper eggs.

Before long
a hungry mole
comes burrowing through the ground.
He is hunting.
He would like a supper
of grasshopper eggs.

The mole finds the eggs.
He eats fourteen of them.
But before he has time
to eat the last one,
a fierce little shrew
darts through the tunnel
and frightens him away.

And then
a grub of the blister beetle
comes scrambling through the grass.
He is hungry.
He would like a supper
of grasshopper eggs.

But
the grub of the blister beetle
burrows down into the ground
and finds another nest
of grasshopper eggs,
before he comes to
the *last* grasshopper egg
by the old fence post.

The last tiny egg
lies safely in its cradle of earth
all winter long.
Cold winds blow.
Snow covers the ground
and makes a white cap
on top of the old fence post.
Inside the egg,
beneath the earth and snow,
a little grasshopper is forming.

After the cold winter passes,
the sun's rays warm the earth,
and the grass grows green again.

Now the little grasshopper is ready
to leave his dark home beneath the ground.
He pushes hard,
and his eggshell bursts open.
But he is still all wrapped up
in a clear, tight skin.
Even so
he wiggles and twists
and pushes and struggles,
until he works his way
up through the ground
that covers him.
At last he pushes his way out into
the light, bright world.

Now he must get out
of his clear, tight skin.
So he pushes hard
with the back of his neck
until the skin breaks open.
At last he is free
to hop and jump.
The tiny grasshopper
has a large head,
six legs,
but no wings as yet.
His two hind legs are red,
long and powerful,
and made just right
for jumping about.

Now away goes the tiny red-legged
grasshopper!
Even though
little Red Legs
is so very tiny
that one would have to look carefully
to see him in the grass,
his first jump is
twenty times
the length of his own body.

Little Red Legs
is very hard to catch
because his five eyes
warn him of danger.
Three small eyes
in the front of his head
see things near him.
Large eyes,
one on each side of his head,
see things farther away.
Two jointed "feelers" on his forehead
tell him how things *smell*.
He can turn them in all directions.
The shorter jointed "feelers"

at the corners of his mouth
tell him how things *taste*.

Red Legs breathes through
little holes
along each side of his body.
These little holes are called *spiracles*.
They make one think of portholes
in a ship.
He has no ears that *look like ears*.
But if one looked closely,
one would find
a clear, round spot
on each side of his body,
above and slightly back of
the places where his hind legs
join his body.

These clear spots are Red Legs' ears.
They look like little windows.

Red Legs stays in sunny fields
where there are grass and clover
and green leaves for food.
He climbs up stems of grass
and nibbles on the blades.
To such a tiny grasshopper,
the grassy jungle
must seem like
a giant forest.

Red Legs eats so much
and grows so fast
that within a week
his outer skin is much too tight.
One sunny day
it splits open along the middle of his back.
He crawls out of it,
leaving his old outgrown skin
lying on the ground.
The new skin
covering Red Legs' body
is soft and moist.
Now he is quite helpless.
He cannot hop about
until his skin is dry and hard again.

While he sits quietly in the sun
waiting for his skin to dry,
a big brown turkey
comes stalking across the meadow.
He is looking for grasshoppers
to gobble for breakfast.
Frightened grasshoppers make zig-zag
jumps,
first this way, then that way.
The brown turkey snaps them up
in his big strong beak
when they are not quick enough
to jump away.
His big foot almost steps on tiny Red Legs
as he passes by.

At last
Red Legs' skin is dry and hard,
and he can jump again.
As the summer days go by,
he eats and grows.
Each week he sheds his skin
for a new and larger one
and then begins again
to eat and grow.
When he has shed his skin four times,
he has little stubby wings
on his back.

It is not easy for Red Legs
to grow up;
there are dangers all about.
A leopard frog,
hiding among the cattails
near the meadow's edge,
tries to catch him.

A tiger salamander,
hiding near a mossy log,
tries to catch him.

And a little sparrow hawk,
darting down from above,
tries to catch him.

But Red Legs sees
the frog,
the salamander,
and the sparrow hawk
in time to hop away.
And so
he lives to shed his skin
the fifth time.
Now he has two pairs of wings,
all moist and crumpled,
and folded along his back.
He spreads his wings
to dry them in the sun.

When his wings are dry,
Red Legs rises above the meadow
like a small airplane.
His stiff upper wings
are spread straight out.

His delicate lower wings,
making a whirring sound,
carry him across the meadow.

He flies over the dusty road,
into a farmer's yard
and lands
to rest among the blades of grass.
He folds his delicate lower wings
along his back
like pleated fans
and covers them
with his strong, hard upper wings.
But here too there is danger.
A toad,
sitting under a bush,
tries to catch him.

The farmer's big gray cat
tries to catch him.

The farmer's little boy,
running through the grass,
tries to catch him,
and
he does!

But
when the farmer's little boy
opens his hand,
Red Legs jumps out
and quickly hops away.

One day Red Legs finds
a lady grasshopper
sitting close to him
nibbling clover.
Like a fiddler playing a fiddle,
he raises one of his strong hind legs
and, using it as a bow,
draws it across his upper wing.
"Zzzzt! Zzzzt! Zzzzt!"
Red Legs fiddles a "song" for her.

She hears the "song"
that Red Legs plays.

It tells her
that he likes her very much.
It is not long before
they spread their wings
and fly away together.
She is Red Legs' mate.

The summer days go by.
Yellow goldenrod
blooms along the fence,
and red sumac
makes gay patches on the hillside
telling that autumn is on the way.

Before the last warm days are gone,
Red Legs' mate finds soft earth
in which to lay her eggs.

She pushes her *egg-placer*
into the soft earth,
making a small hole.
There she hides her tiny eggs.

Red Legs and his mate
will not be in the meadow next spring,
for red-legged grasshoppers live their lives
in one short summer.
But
from the eggs
hidden in the ground
there will come
other red-legged grasshoppers
that will
eat and grow and hop about
as Red Legs did.